Title:Lets Look at Armadill
R.L.:2.3
PTS:0.5
TST:138520

D1272368

LIGHTNING BOLT BOOKS™

Let's Look at Armadillos

Jackson County Public Library
Seymour, Indiana 47274

WITHDRAWN

Judith Jango-Cohen

Lerner Publications Company
Minneapolis

Copyright © 2011 by Judith Jango-Cohen

All rights reserved. International copyright secured. No part of this book may be reproduced, stored in a retrieval system, or transmitted in any form or by any means—electronic, mechanical, photocopying, recording, or otherwise—without the prior written permission of Lerner Publishing Group, Inc., except for the inclusion of brief quotations in an acknowledged review.

Lerner Publications Company
A division of Lerner Publishing Group, Inc.
241 First Avenue North
Minneapolis, MN 55401 U.S.A.

Website address: www.lernerbooks.com

Library of Congress Cataloging-in-Publication Data

Jango-Cohen, Judith.
    Let's look at armadillos / by Judith Jango-Cohen.
        p.   cm. — (Lightning bolt books™—Animal close-ups)
    Includes index.
    ISBN 978-0-7613-3887-1 (lib. bdg. : alk. paper)
    1. Armadillos—Juvenile literature. I. Title.
  QL737.E23J254 2011
  599.3′12—dc22   2009038457

Manufactured in the United States of America
1 — CG — 7/15/10

Contents

Digging Armadillos

Why is this animal digging? This is an armadillo. Armadillos dig for many reasons. Digging helps them stay alive.

SNIFF! GRUNT!

This armadillo is
smelling the ground.

Do you know why?

Armadillos can smell bugs under the ground. They dig to find the bugs.

Two armadillos dig in the dirt to search for food.

Then they lick up the bugs with their long, sticky tongues.

SLURP!

Armadillos like bugs best,
but they eat plants too.
Armadillos are omnivores.

Omnivores are animals that eat both plants and animals. **Are you an omnivore?**

This armadillo eats an earthworm.

Danger!

This armadillo is smelling the air to find out if a predator is near. A predator is an animal that hunts and eats other animals.

Oh no! A dog is hunting nearby. ZIP! The armadillo runs away.

What if it cannot run faster than a predator?

The predator might try to bite. A hard shell called a carapace protects the armadillo's body.

This is the armadillo's carapace.

How can an armadillo move around in such a hard shell?

A carapace has many
thin bands in the middle.

Count the bands in the
carapace of this armadillo.

Bands help a carapace bend.

A Great Escape

A carapace is heavy. To escape from a predator, an armadillo may need to swim. How can it swim without sinking?

The armadillo swallows lots of air. The air helps the armadillo float. How else can armadillos escape from predators?

Air helps this armadillo swim through the water.

They dig! SCRITCH-SCRATCH! Quick as a flash, an armadillo digs a small hole and hides inside.

An armadillo tunnels into the ground to stay safe.

Sharp claws help an armadillo dig quickly.

19

An armadillo holds its
breath as it digs to keep
dirt out of its nose.

An armadillo can also dig a
big hole called a den.
A den is a safe place where an
armadillo can rest.

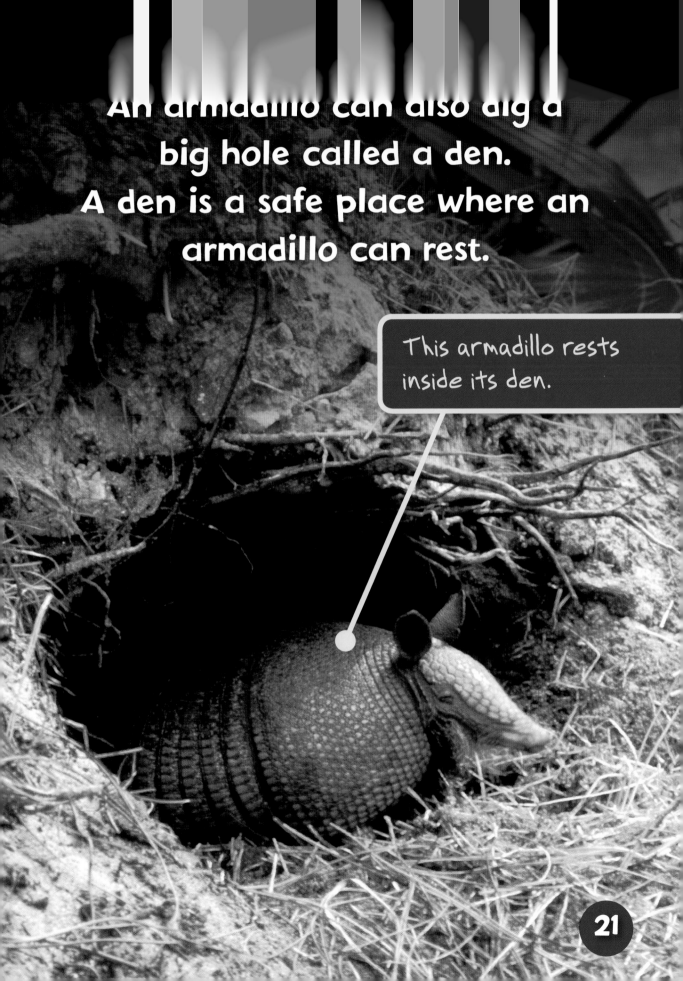

This armadillo rests
inside its den.

Pups

A den also makes a cozy nest for babies. Armadillo babies are called pups.

A newborn pup can see
and hear. It has a soft pink
carapace.

Do you know which
armadillo is the pup?

On the day it is born, a pup can walk, climb, and play. As it grows up, its carapace will become hard and gray.

This newborn pup climbs on dirt.

Armadillos belong to a group of animals called mammals. Like all baby mammals, armadillo pups drink milk from their mother.

Four armadillo pups drink milk from their mother.

When pups are older, they leave their den to hunt for food.

This pup hunts for food in the soil with its nose.

Armadillos are amazing.
They run, swim, hunt, grunt,
sniff, and lick.
Most of all, they dig!

Armadillos are great
diggers!

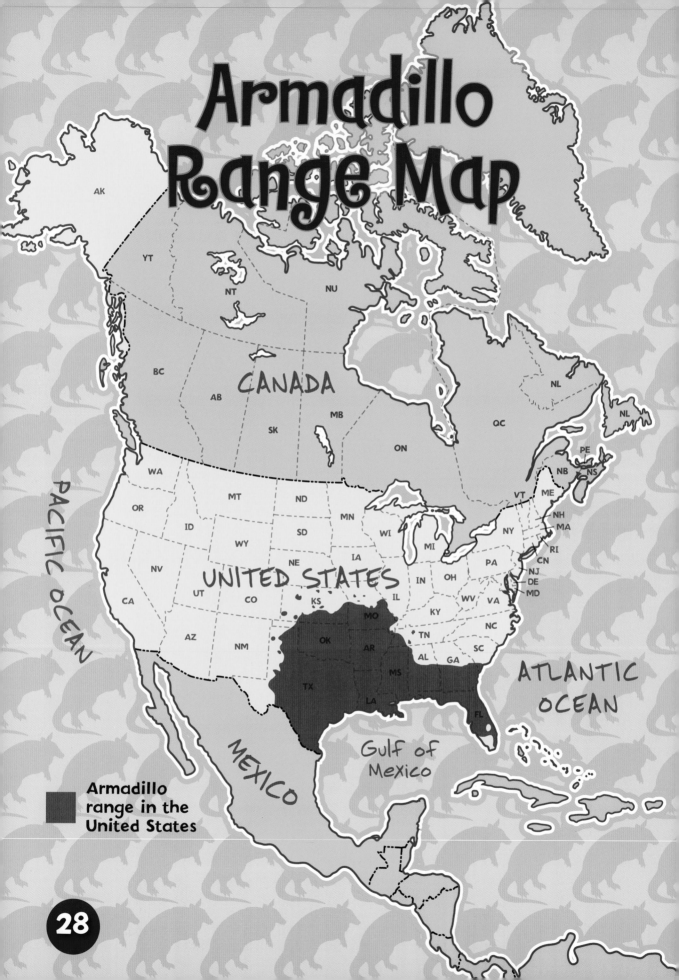

Armadillo Range Map

AK

YT

NT

NU

BC

AB

CANADA

SK

MB

ON

QC

NL

NL

PE

NB

NS

WA

MT

ND

MN

VT

ME

OR

ID

SD

WI

NH

MA

WY

NE

IA

MI

NY

RI

CN

NV

UNITED STATES

IN

OH

PA

NJ
DE

CA

UT

CO

KS

IL

WV

VA

MD

MO

KY

AZ

NM

OK

AR

TN

NC

SC

AL

GA

ATLANTIC
OCEAN

TX

MS

LA

FL

PACIFIC OCEAN

MEXICO

Gulf of
Mexico

Armadillo
range in the
United States

Armadillo Diagram

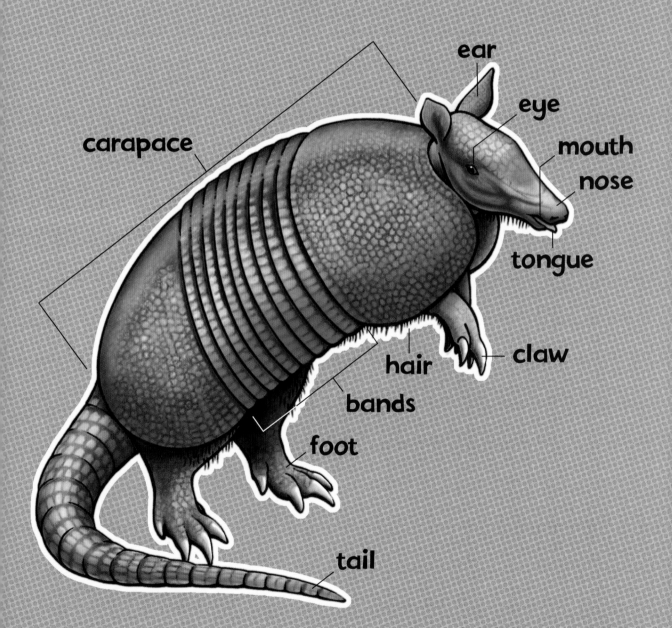

ear

eye

mouth

nose

tongue

carapace

claw

hair

bands

foot

tail

Glossary

carapace: the hard shell that covers the body of an armadillo

den: a cozy, safe place to live

mammal: an animal that has hair and drinks its mother's milk when young. Humans, wolves, bats, and whales are mammals.

omnivore: an animal that eats both plants and animals

predator: an animal that hunts and eats other animals

pup: a baby armadillo

Further Reading

Animal Bytes: Armadillos
http://www.sandiegozoo.org/animalbytes/t-armadillo.html

Enchanted Learning: Armadillos
http://www.enchantedlearning.com/subjects/mammals/armadillo/Armadilloprintout.shtml

Jango-Cohen, Judith. *Armadillos.* New York: Benchmark Books, 2004.

McKerley, Jennifer Guess. *Amazing Armadillos.* New York: Random House, 2009.

National Geographic: Armadillos
http://animals.nationalgeographic.com/animals/mammals/armadillo.html

Swinburne, Stephen R. *Armadillo Trail: The Northward Journey of the Armadillo.* Honesdale, PA: Boyds Mills Press, 2009.

Index

Photo Acknowledgments

The images in this book are used with the permission of: © Joel Sartore/National Geographic/Getty Images, pp. 1, 30, 31; © Larry Ditto/Photoshot, pp. 2, 4; © Heidi & Hans-Juergen Koch/Minden Pictures, pp. 5, 12, 16, 19, 24, 26; © Martin Harvey/Peter Arnold, Inc., p. 6; © Bianca Lavies/National Geographic/Getty Images, pp. 7, 22, 25; © Richard Goff, p. 8; © Bruce Coleman/Allan Blank/Photoshot, p. 9; © Rolf Nussbaumer Photography/Alamy, p. 10; © Bill Draker/Rolf Nussbaumer Photography/Alamy, pp. 11, 15; © Stephen J. Krasemann/Photolibrary, p. 13; © Fred Whitehead/Animals Animals, pp. 14, 18; © Claus Meyer/Minden Pictures, p. 17; © Ilene MacDonald/Alamy, p. 20; © Jeff Foott/Photoshot, p. 21; © Jeff Foott/Discovery Channel Images/Getty Images, p. 23; © Gerry Bishop/Visuals Unlimited, Inc., p. 27; © Laura Westlund/Independent Picture Service, pp. 28, 29.

Front cover: © Heidi & Hans-Juergen Koch/Minden Pictures.